KU-244-332

World Wildlife Fund

Jillian Powell

W

FRANKLIN WATTS
LONDON•SYDNEY

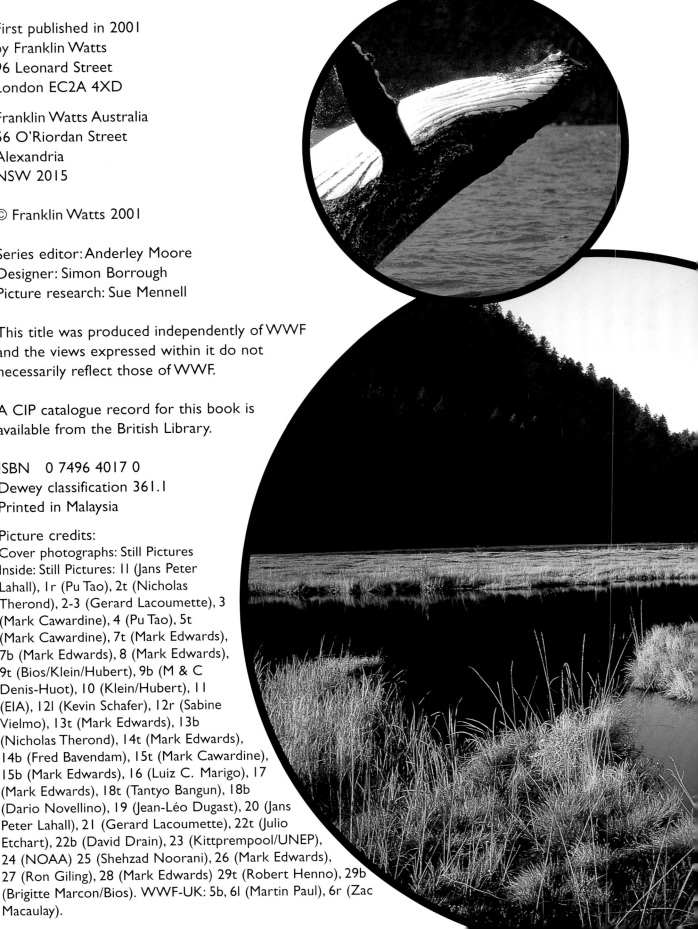

First published in 2001
by Franklin Watts
96 Leonard Street
London EC2A 4XD

Franklin Watts Australia
56 O'Riordan Street
Alexandria
NSW 2015

Series editor: Anderley Moore
Designer: Simon Borrough
Picture research: Sue Mennell

This title was produced independently of WWF
and the views expressed within it do not
necessarily reflect those of WWF.

A CIP catalogue record for this book is
available from the British Library.

ISBN   0 7496 4017 0
Dewey classification 361.1
Printed in Malaysia

Picture credits:
Cover photographs: Still Pictures
Inside: Still Pictures: 1l (Jans Peter
Lahall), 1r (Pu Tao), 2t (Nicholas
Therond), 2-3 (Gerard Lacoumette), 3
(Mark Cawardine), 4 (Pu Tao), 5t
(Mark Cawardine), 7t (Mark Edwards),
7b (Mark Edwards), 8 (Mark Edwards),
9t (Bios/Klein/Hubert), 9b (M & C
Denis-Huot), 10 (Klein/Hubert), 11
(EIA), 12l (Kevin Schafer), 12r (Sabine
Vielmo), 13t (Mark Edwards), 13b
(Nicholas Therond), 14t (Mark Edwards),
14b (Fred Bavendam), 15t (Mark Cawardine),
15b (Mark Edwards), 16 (Luiz C. Marigo), 17
(Mark Edwards), 18t (Tantyo Bangun), 18b
(Dario Novellino), 19 (Jean-Léo Dugast), 20 (Jans
Peter Lahall), 21 (Gerard Lacoumette), 22t (Julio
Etchart), 22b (David Drain), 23 (Kittprempool/UNEP),
24 (NOAA) 25 (Shehzad Noorani), 26 (Mark Edwards),
27 (Ron Giling), 28 (Mark Edwards) 29t (Robert Henno), 29b
(Brigitte Marcon/Bios). WWF-UK: 5b, 6l (Martin Paul), 6r (Zac
Macaulay).

The World Wildlife Fund is the world's largest nature conservation organization. It has nearly 5 million members and is active in about 100 countries. WWF campaigns to protect biodiversity (the variety of life on Earth), to reduce pollution and waste, and to encourage sustainable development (finding ways of doing things that do not damage the environment or exhaust natural resources).

WWF's main aims are: to protect and conserve endangered species and address global threats to nature by seeking long-term solutions to the planet's environmental problems.

 Checklist

WWF aims to protect these natural habitats and all the species that live in them by:

- raising funds for conservation projects world wide
- creating protected areas
- lobbying governments on environmental issues
- providing scientific expertise
- researching and campaigning to raise environmental levels of environmental awareness

▼ *This panda in the Wolong Nature Reserve in China is protected as part of WWF's Operation Panda.*

 Checklist

1948 The IUCN – now the World Conservation Union – is set up

1961 WWF is set up after the Morges Manifesto is signed by world conservation experts.

1986 WWF adopts the name World Wide Fund for Nature, except in the US and Canada where it remains the World Wildlife Fund.

1992 The Earth Summit – the world's first global conference on the environment – is held in Rio de Janeiro, Brazil.

Origins

WWF was formed in 1961 and was the first international organization that set out to save endangered wildlife world wide. Its work began when wildlife experts became worried about the fall in the number of wild animals in western Africa, which could lead to their extinction if not stopped. The naturalist Sir Peter Scott was then Vice President of the IUCN, an organization which researched and collected data on nature conservation. He suggested that a new organization should be set up to raise funds for conservation projects, working in partnership with the IUCN. This became the World Wildlife Fund (WWF). Its first campaigns included projects to save endangered species like the tiger and the rhinoceros.

By 1980, WWF had announced a new World Conservation Strategy. Its policies and campaigns expanded from the protection of species and natural habitats, to include issues such as sustainable farming and energy, global warming and climate change.

▲ *The Northern White Rhino, Zaire — the world's rarest rhino and a seriously endangered species.*

Spotlight

In the late 1950s, hundreds of people visited London Zoo to see the Giant Panda Chi-Chi. At that time, pandas were one of the species that were in danger of becoming extinct, which is why Chi-Chi was chosen as the logo for WWF, designed by Sir Peter Scott

Spotlight

Tony Cunningham is the Africa Regional Co-ordinator for WWF's People and Plants project. He has helped identify sites that are important habitats for plants and animals and campaigned for alternatives to wild plants that have become endangered. People and Plants works with local people in Africa and other countries to protect the variety of plant life and develop sustainable harvesting of plants

WWF has its headquarters in Gland, Switzerland, where its staff, the Secretariat, are based. Around the world, it has a network of organizations that help manage its activities. The national organizations, like **WWF-UK**, and **WWF-US**, are all independent, but they work closely together on global projects. Programme offices carry out fieldwork, advise local and national governments and educate local communities on conservation issues.

▼ *Sponsored events raise awareness and funds for WWF campaigns.*

Funding

Almost half of WWF's income comes from its membership fees and another 13 per cent comes from money left in wills or as gifts. The national offices raise funds to run projects in their own countries, and richer ones contribute about two-thirds of their income to global conservation programmes. Volunteers around the world help with fundraising by organizing activities such as sponsored events. WWF also receives income from government grants and aid agencies. WWF raises funds through partnerships with business and industry. Another source of funding is the 1001 Nature Trust. This is made up of 1001 individuals who have given large sums of money to the organization.

● Spotlight

Volunteers play an important part in fundraising for WWF by taking part in sponsored events like bicycle rides, walks and swims. In 1999, over 5000 people in the UK took part in a Great WWF Shark Swim to raise funds for the shark and other endangered marine species. Many species of shark could become extinct because they are hunted for their meat, liver, oil and fins.

Team work

WWF works as an independent, non party-political organization. It runs conservation projects in partnership with governments, international organizations and aid agencies, non-governmental organizations, businesses and local communities.

▲ *Local fishermen attend a WWF workshop on sustainable fishing practices in the Banc D'Arguin National Park, Mauretania.*

One of the WWF's many conservation programmes involved working with the government of Peru and the Peruvian Association for the Protection of Nature (APECO) to protect Manu National Park. WWF provided rangers, jeeps and equipment to protect the park from settlers. The project engaged local people in tree- and crop-planting schemes, helping them to develop sustainable farming methods. WWF recognises that involving local people is vital to the success of any conservation programme. Often, they are facing difficulties such as a shortage of food or water, which have to be overcome first for conservation to succeed.

▲ *As part of a conservation programme in Nigeria, local people harvest new crops that have been grown on deforested land.*

Co-operation between WWF and local people for the sake of the environment has not only affected rainforest areas and other land habitats, but also benefited the world's oceans. WWF has worked with people from various nations to try and reduce the number of nations fishing international waters for their fish quota. Through its policy of monitoring the number of species in all environments, WWF became aware of the serious decline in numbers of various species of fish used in the food industry. It has warned all nations of the dangers of overfishing in certain waters, and by working in collaboration with the countries involved, has put measures in place to lessen the risk of extinction to endangered marine species.

 Spotlight

In the 1970s and 80s, there was so much over-fishing that some stocks, such as the herring fisheries in the North Sea, were almost exhausted. In 1996, WWF worked in partnership with Unilever, the world's largest buyer of frozen fish, to set up the Marine Stewardship Council (MSC). This is a scheme that aims to conserve endangered fish stocks by using the MSC mark to show which fish have come from sustainable fisheries.

 Spotlight

WWF's Endangered Seas Campaign has been working with people in the Galapagos Islands and Mauretania to improve marine protected areas. They have created no-take zones and taught native fishermen sustainable fishing methods in order to try and prevent fish stocks from being exhausted.

Imaraguen fishermen from Mauretania fish for golden mullet. WWF has taught them to use nets that do not trap young fish, helping them practise sustainable fishing methods.

3. Species conservation

We share our planet with about 1.8 million known animal and plant species. But scientists believe that we may only have discovered about one-seventh of all the species on Earth. They call the variety of life on Earth biodiversity. WWF has made the protection of biodiversity one of its main aims.

Scientists estimate that about 6,500 animal species and over 30,000 plant species are currently endangered and could become extinct. Many animal species are endangered because of hunting, or illegal poaching. They include tigers, rhinos and elephants. They are hunted for their skins, bones, horns and other animal parts that are used to make clothes, jewellery or traditional types of medicine, which some people believe cure disease. They may also be endangered because their natural habitat is being destroyed for farming or development.

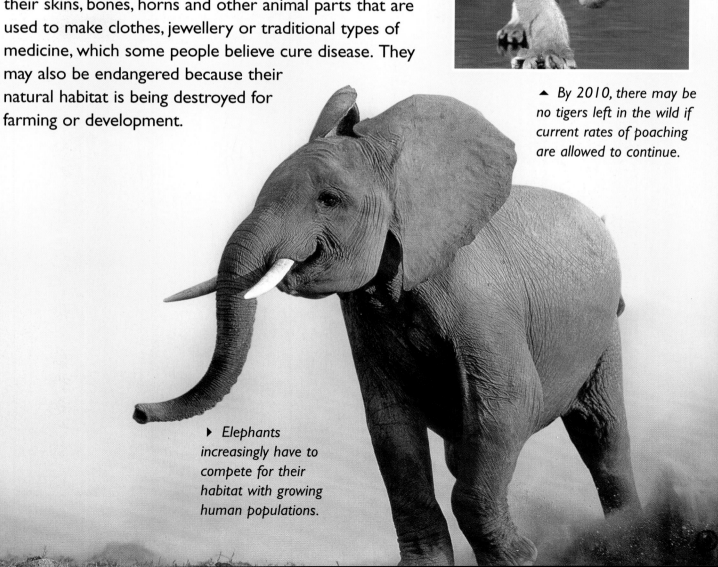

▲ *By 2010, there may be no tigers left in the wild if current rates of poaching are allowed to continue.*

▶ *Elephants increasingly have to compete for their habitat with growing human populations.*

● Spotlight

WWF is working on a project to protect Indonesia's endangered Javan rhino in the Ujung Kulon National Park. There are only about 47 Javan rhinos remaining in the wild in Indonesia. They live in thick forests but local people were cutting down trees for firewood, destroying their habitat. WWF is helping the people to grow crops like ginger to give them an income, and to plant more trees to supply the wood they need for fuel and cooking.

▼ *The Snow Leopard is endangered by hunting for its fur and also by falling numbers of its prey, such as wild sheep and goats.*

Biodiversity

We are facing the greatest extinction of animals and plants on Earth since the dinosaurs died out 65 million years ago. Biodiversity is an important part of the natural balance of our planet. WWF aims to protect all species by creating protected wildlife areas and by planting and protecting more forests. WWF works with local communities to protect wildlife and educate people on the importance of biodiversity. It campaigns against the trade in animal parts and funds anti-poaching teams and equipment.

Stopping trade in endangered species

There are already controls on wildlife trade through CITES, the Convention on International Trade in Endangered Species. The illegal trade in wildlife is thought to be worth about $20 billion a year. It includes animal furs, ivory, exotic animals for the pet market, plants and fish. In 1976, WWF and the IUCN set up TRAFFIC, a watchdog organization for trade in wildlife. Its staff work through a network of 21 offices, sometimes as under-cover investigators.

▲ *Amazon parrots are caged for export from Argentina as part of the trade in exotic pets.*

In 1979, WWF set up Operation Panda in the Wolong Nature Reserve, a breeding station and research unit in China. Pandas are endangered because of poaching, the destruction of their natural habitat and a shortage of bamboo, which is their only food. WWF is funding the planting of bamboo corridors so that pandas can move from one protected area to another to find more food.

In 1971, there were around 65,000 black rhinos in Africa. By the 1990s, just 3000 were left. Trade in rhino horn is illegal, but a poacher can earn enough money from one horn to feed his family for months. When people are faced with problems of poverty, conservation issues may not seem important to them. WWF works with local people to educate them on the importance of conservation and help them find ways of making a living without poaching.

◄ *The Giant Panda is at risk because of a shortage of bamboo.*

▶ *These illegal supplies of ivory and animal pelts intended for trade on the black market were seized by officials in Tanzania.*

● Spotlight

Botanist Reza Azmi is WWF's scientific officer working on a WWF-Malaysia project to preserve the biodiversity of plants in the country. Reza collects specimens of plants which he identifies and catalogues. His studies of plants and their natural habitats will lead to a better understanding of which species are endangered and the major threats to their habitats.

Oceans and seas cover 70 per cent of our planet, but only a tiny fraction are protected areas. In the last 50 years, marine life has come under threat from pollution, over-fishing and coastal development.

WWF's marine policies aim to create a global network of marine protected areas, to promote good coastal management and to reduce and stop marine pollution. They also work to encourage sustainable fishing practices and conserve endangered marine species.

▲ Sand eel are landed at Esbjerg in Denmark. They are one of many species endangered by over-fishing in the North Sea.

▲ Killing with harpoons and dynamite has brought many whale species, including the Humpback, close to extinction.

 Problem

The International Whaling Commission (IWC) has failed to stop the hunting of whales. Countries including Japan and Norway have continued to hunt species like the minke whale, claiming that they do so for scientific purposes. Since 1992, the number of whales killed every year has been rising, and the IWC is now facing a crisis as these countries are constantly trying to find new ways of justifying their actions and challenging its powers.

WWF researches and reports on problems that affect marine life. It also campaigns for better controls of trade in marine species through international agreements between countries fishing the same waters, and for changes to fishing equipment. These include the kind of nets that can trap and kill marine creatures such as dolphins, turtles and porpoises.

▲ A patrol boat funded by WWF guards the fisheries in the Banc D'Arguin National Park in Mauretania to prevent illegal fishing by large trawlers.

▲ Coral reefs are rich marine habitats. Many are now endangered by pollution and by changes due to global warming.

Save the whale

By the middle of the last century the use of harpoons and dynamite had destroyed many species of whale, and seven out of eleven species of great whale were close to extinction. In the 1970s, hundreds of people joined anti-whaling rallies and campaigns to Save the Whale yet some countries have continued to hunt them.

▲ *The enormous and powerful tail of a sperm whale – one of the endangered great whale species.*

● Spotlight

Phang-Nga Bay in Thailand is under threat from trawlers and other large fishing vessels that ignore local fishing regulations and fines and are exhausting fish stocks. WWF is working with local communities to help protect the area, which includes mangroves and seagrass habitats. It has funded a team of field workers and is giving practical help in managing the coast and enforcing fishing regulations.

▼ *A mangrove forest in Thailand. More than 50 per cent of these forests have been destroyed for shrimp farming.*

Forests are home to over half of the world's animal and plant species, and scientists believe they may contain hundreds of thousands more species still to be discovered.

Forests help balance our planet's climate. Trees absorb carbon dioxide and pump out oxygen, acting as the planet's lungs. They also recycle rainfall, preventing floods and droughts. But every year, millions of hectares of the world's forests are being destroyed for ever, for timber or firewood or to clear land for farming or development. Scientists estimate that the world has already lost up to two-thirds of its forests, and by 2050 there may be no natural forests left in countries such as Indonesia, Malaysia and Costa Rica.

▼ An aerial view of the Amazon rainforest in Brazil. WWF and the World Bank are working together to protect 25 million hectares of Brazilian forest.

◑ Problem

In 1997, forest fires in Indonesia destroyed vast areas of natural forest and caused a poisonous smog to cover much of the country, killing endangered wildlife including orang utans and rhinos. These fires are believed to have been started illegally by logging companies to clear the land quickly. WWF is lobbying governments in the region to change policies such as giving subsidies for logging and agriculture that encourage the burning of forests. WWF is also campaigning for an International Court of the Environment to be set up which could help prevent illegal logging and fire raising.

▼ *Forest fires like this one in Brazil create pollution, erode the soil and ruin the local ecology. Some fires are thought to have been set on purpose to clear land for cattle ranches.*

▲ *A meeting in Indonesia to co-ordinate emergency action to try and stop the increasing number of forest fires.*

WWF has campaigned to save the world's tropical rainforests since 1975. Today, its Forests for Life programme supports over 300 projects in more than 65 countries. It aims to set up a network of protected areas (just 6 per cent of the world's forests are currently protected) and to encourage good forest management outside protected areas. It is also working to develop programmes to restore forests and to reduce forest damage from climate change and pollution.

 Spotlight

The forests of the Northern Andes in South America are home to over 200 bird species and 86 species of palm tree, including the world's tallest palm, the wax palm. The area is threatened by farming, ranching, logging and mining, and at least 55 per cent of its forests have been lost. WWF has sent a team of experts to the area. They have drawn up maps showing areas of forest, patterns of land use and population, and are developing a conservation plan to protect the remaining forest.

▼ *Logging in the forest of Riau in Sumatra, Indonesia.*

The Forest Stewardship Council

In 1993, WWF joined other conservation groups and timber companies to form the Forest Stewardship Council. The FSC sets standards for sustainable forest management. Companies agree to buy and sell only from well-managed forests, and the public can choose to buy timber products with the FSC trademark.

▸ *A harvest of bamboo is transported by raft down a river in Sulawesi, Indonesia.*

 Spotlight

In Quintana Roo, Mexico, WWF is helping local Mayan peoples to manage 150,000 hectares of forest in sustainable ways. They run their own saw mills and sell forest products including timber, pepper and honey through a workers' co-operative. This means that the local people have an income from the forest and have an interest in protecting it.

6. Freshwater and wetland conservation

Wetlands cover just 6 per cent of the Earth's surface but they are vital to the natural balance of our planet. They include mangrove swamps, marshes, estuaries, tidal flats and shallow seas. Wetlands add to and purify the Earth's water reserves and help protect coastal areas. They are also important wildlife habitats.

▲ An aerial view of the Rapadalen Delta in Sweden. Deltas, where rivers meet the sea, provide a fertile wetland habitat.

Many of the world's wetlands are under threat. They are being damaged by rising sea levels due to global warming and by pollution from chemicals like pesticides being washed into rivers. Others are lost because of land drainage for farming or river engineering schemes. Some countries have already lost between 50 to 80 per cent of their wetlands.

Problem

Dams and embankments can help provide water and energy for a growing population, but they can also endanger or destroy precious wetlands. In Iceland, there are plans to flood up to 180 square kilometres of wilderness in Snaefell. Reservoirs will be linked by tunnels to a power station which will power the production of aluminium. WWF is campaigning to protect the area as a national park because it provides a natural habitat for around 3000 reindeer, 310 plant species and dozens of species of birds. Some people support the reservoir project because it would bring 500 new jobs to the area. But many people oppose the project. WWF is working with INCA, the Iceland National Conservation Association, to call for a report looking at how the development would affect the environment.

In 1971, over 100 countries signed the Ramsar Convention which pledged to protect threatened wetlands. Over 1000 valuable wetland sites are now protected. WWF launched its Wetlands Conservation Fund in 1990, to fund projects to conserve wetlands under threat in developing countries. WWF experts advise local governments, prepare wetland conservation and management plans and train people to become wetland rangers. WWF is building databases of wetland sites.

▼ A peat bog in the Vosges mountains in France. Peat bogs are ancient wildlife habitats.

The water crisis

Water covers two-thirds of our planet's surface but only 2.5 per cent of that is freshwater. Most of it is found as groundwater or in the polar ice-caps and glaciers, leaving only a tiny fraction available in lakes and rivers. About 1.3 billion people in the world today don't have access to safe drinking water, and United Nations experts predict that by 2025, two-thirds of the world's population could face serious water shortages. The water crisis is caused by natural factors such as drought but also by pollution and poor water management.

WWF's Freshwater Programme, and the Endangered Seas Campaign, launched in 1999, aim to protect freshwater reserves for people and the environment.

▲ A beach in Venezuela, polluted by rubbish left by tourists.

▼ The North Sea is polluted by the dumping of sewage and other waste matter.

7. Climate change

In the 1970s, scientists began to report changes in the Earth's climate. They detected a 'greenhouse effect', which was warming up the Earth's temperature. Waste gases from cars and industry, including carbon dioxide, were trapping heat from the sun in the Earth's atmosphere, leading to global warming.

▲ *Parched earth in Thailand shows the effects of severe drought.*

They also began to detect holes in the ozone layer which protects the planet from the sun's dangerous rays. These were being caused by the effect of chemicals polluting the Earth's atmosphere. Records show that the tropics are getting hotter and drier, and the Sahara Desert is expanding. The Antarctic and Arctic ice sheets are breaking up and as a result, sea levels are an average 20 centimetres higher world wide than they were 100 years ago. Around 80 per cent of the world's beaches are now being worn away by rising sea levels.

Some scientists predict that sea levels will rise by up to half a metre by the end of this century, if the greenhouse effect goes on increasing. Most scientists now agree that global warming could have disastrous effects on the human population and the environment. There will be more extremes of weather, such as droughts, floods, storms and hurricanes. Diseases such as malaria could spread in a warmer climate to affect up to a third of the world's population.

▼ *Violent weather effects such as tornadoes are becoming more frequent due to global warming.*

 Spotlight

WWF–Netherlands worked with five of the largest building firms in the country on a scheme to build 200 energy-efficient homes. It is also working with Swiss and American technology firms to develop solar power for heating and lighting.

▲ Rising sea levels are leading to devastating floods in low-lying countries like Bangladesh.

 Spotlight

In Poland, the country's poor energy efficiency meant that for every hour of electricity used, three times more carbon dioxide was being produced than in Germany. WWF has been funding projects to make Polish people aware of the hazards of wasting energy. Schools and businesses have been sent information packs on how to save energy in the home, such as using low-energy light bulbs.

The Climate Change Campaign

WWF launched its Climate Change Campaign in the 1990s. The main goal of the campaign is to protect the environment by reducing levels of greenhouse gases in the atmosphere. WWF is lobbying governments to take steps to achieve this. Measures include switching from fossil fuels (oil, coal, gas) to clean, sustainable sources of energy such as wind, wave and solar power, cutting energy waste, investing in public transport to reduce the number of cars on the roads, and making industry pay a climate-change tax.

Forest preservation and climate change

Another way to reduce global warming is to stop the destruction of forests, which absorb carbon dioxide from the Earth's atmosphere. Scientists believe that the loss of forests could add up to 10 billion tonnes of carbon dioxide to the Earth's atmosphere every year.

▲ Forest workers in Brazil take mahogany tree seedlings to be planted in areas of rainforest that have been damaged. It takes twenty five years for mahogany trees to reach maturity.

Since WWF was founded, the human population has almost doubled to more than 6 billion people. Every year, more forest, farmland and wildlife habitats are lost to development. Pollution has increased and is leading to changes in the global climate. Water reserves are falling and areas of desert increasing. Experts believe that the human population will more than double again by the middle of the twenty-first century, putting more of a strain on the Earth's natural resources.

▲ In the Americas and Europe, about seven in ten people live in cities. Cities such as La Paz in Bolivia, shown here, are among the most densely populated areas of the world.

◑ Problem

By 2000, half the world's population was living in cities. Cities take up just 2 per cent of the Earth's land surface, but use 75 per cent of its resources. In future, just supplying enough fresh water to the world's growing cities could be a major challenge. WWF has produced a report making recommendations for new measures, such as planting more forests, rainwater harvesting, and educating local communities on water management and conservation.

WWF estimates that people have destroyed over 30 per cent of the natural world since 1970. But now there are signs that we are at last becoming more aware of the problems facing the environment.

In 1992, 160 countries and conservation groups met together for the world's biggest ever conference on the environment. It was called the Earth Summit. The world's nations agreed to try and reduce global warming, and protect biodiversity. In the 1990s, WWF announced its new programme 'Caring for the Earth', focusing on conservation of forests, freshwater systems, and oceans and coasts.

▲ The Tree of Life sculpture at the United Nations Earth Summit held in Rio, Brazil in 1992. WWF was one of many conservation organizations that attended the summit.

Future problems

WWF and other conservation groups face major challenges in the twenty-first century. They include a growing human population and an increasing gap between rich and poor countries. As pollution increases, and natural resources and fossil fuels run out, there could also be disastrous changes in climate due to rising sea levels.

WWF and the future

Without WWF, many species, including tigers, rhinos, polar bears and whales might already have become extinct, and the world would have lost even more of its precious resources like tropical rainforests and wetland habitats. But as the Earth enters a new millennium, nature conservation has never been a greater challenge than it is now.

▲ *Polar bears in the Arctic are one of many species threatened by the effects of global warming.*

▼ *Warmer temperatures are breaking up ice sheets and glaciers, leading to rising sea levels.*

Spotlight

Antarctica has been described as the Earth's last wilderness. As well as being an important wildlife habitat, it helps scientists measure changes in the environment. But in the 1980s, Antarctica came under threat from countries wanting to mine for precious minerals including oil, gold and silver. A conservation plan to save Antarctica was launched and in 1991, an international agreement was reached to protect it from oil and mineral exploration for at least half a century.

Glossary

biodiversity — the variety of life on Earth

commercial — carried out on a big scale for profit

deforestation — cutting down forests

endangered — in danger of becoming extinct

extinct — died out completely, as in a species

fossil fuels — natural fuels such as coal, oil and gas that are the fossilized remains of long-dead living things

global warming — the increase in the Earth's temperature due to the effect of pollution in the atmosphere

greenhouse effect — the term scientists use to describe gases that trap heat in the Earth's atmosphere, leading to global warming

habitat — the natural environment of a plant, animal, or person

intensive farming — farming methods designed to produce the maximum amount of yield from a piece of land

nature conservation — protecting and managing the Earth and its environment and natural resources

ozone layer — a layer of gas in the Earth's upper atmosphere that protects it from the sun's harmful rays

pesticides — chemicals used to kill insects or other pests that can cause extensive damage to crops. Used widely in intensive farming

subsidies — grants paid by governments

sustainable — describing a method that does not damage the environment or exhaust natural resources

Useful information

World Wide Fund For Nature
(formerly World Wildlife Fund) International,
Avenue du Mont-Blanc,
CH 1196 Gland,
Switzerland

WWF-UK,
Panda House,
Weyside Park
Godalming,
Surrey, GU7 1XR

WWF international website: www.panda.org

WWF-UK website: www.wwf-uk.org

WWF-US website
www.worldwildlife.org

Become a campaigner for conservation:
If you have access to the Internet look up
the website for online campaigners and apply
for a WWF panda passport at:
www.passport.panda.org
or find out more about these organizations

WSPA
Join the Rangers at WSPA (World Society for
the Protection of Animals)
WSPA,
Dept 1R1,
Freepost,
Melksham, SN12 6GZ
e mail: wspa@wspa.org.uk

Greenpeace UK,
Canonbury Villas,
London N1 2PN
www.greenpeace.org

Friends of the Earth,
26–28 Underwood Street,
London N1 7JQ
www.foe.co.uk